THE PRACTICAL PUPPY BOOTCAMP

Week One

Print ISBN: 978-1-7366280-0-3
eBook ISBN: 978-1-7366280-1-0

Editor: Rochelle Woods
Proofreader: Andi L Gregory
Formatters: Ljiljana Pavkov, Jordan Wade
Cover: Tim Wade
Photographers: Jordan Wade, Anna Sundholm, Tim Wade, Mint_Images/EnvatoElements

Table of Contents

Introduction 7
How to Use This Book 10

Training Prep

Puppy Personalities 14
Training Theory 16
The Structure of Training 18
When and What to Treat 21
Training Session Length 24
Your Training Space 26
Verbal and Physical Cues 27
Lure or Offer 28
Yes and No 30
Shaping Work 32
Stress Behaviors 33
Food Motivation 36
Socialization 38

Training: Week One

The End Goals 42
Day One 44
    Day One Checklist 54
Day Two 55
    Day Two Checklist 64

Day Three 65
    Day Three Checklist 71
Day Four 72
    Day Four Checklist 75
Day Five 76
    Day Five Checklist 80
Day Six 81
    Day Six Checklist 85
Day Seven 86
    Day Seven Checklist 89

Congratulations on completing Week One
    of Puppy Bootcamp! 90
Graduation Test! 91
About the Author 94

THE PRACTICAL PUPPY BOOTCAMP

Introduction

Welcome to the Practical Puppy Bootcamp Week One! If you just received your first puppy and want to train them yourself, or if you've trained your own dog before and are looking for a little more guidance or structure this time around, this booklet is for you!

I'm Jordan Wade, the owner of Practical Puppy Training and co-creator of the YouTube channel The Practical Puppy. The world of dogs has been a lifetime affair for me. I started out working for a kennel-free breeder of service and therapy dogs. I learned to

The Practical Puppy

assess each puppy's temperament for service or therapy potential, and to match them with their forever homes.

Puppies I helped select from litters went on to work for Guide Dogs for the Blind, work in the court system as abused children therapy dogs, or become blood sugar alert dogs, wheelchair assist dogs, etc.

As time went on I stepped into the training role, and began the adventure of developing the Practical Puppy Bootcamp. I've trained dozens of puppies using my program, and all of them have been able to achieve the goals we set in this booklet. I'm confident that it works, and works well. You can see the results for yourself in videos on my website: PracticalPuppyTraining.com

Sometimes following written training instructions can be more difficult than watching a trainer in person. That's why this booklet has links to 20 videos of me training puppies the same way you will be training your new little one! I'll explain how to access them in the next section.

This booklet will walk you through the first week of Puppy Boot-camp. If you follow the program, you will not only give your puppy a good start in cues, socialization, house manners, and learning to have a calm and confident state of mind, but it will also help you navigate potty and crate training.

Once a puppy has completed the first month of my Bootcamp, they are well on their way to being able to take the CGC (Canine Good Citizen) test.

During the first week of Bootcamp, your puppy will be intro-duced and responding to these cues:

- Sit
- Lay Down
- Place
- Leave It

- Look
- Touch
- Kennel Up
- Here

As well as:

- Walking on the Leash
- Food Manners
- Crate Training

- Grooming
- Socialization
- Potty Training

See the end results for yourself in this video!

But before your new puppy comes home and you start working with them, there are some things you need to know. Like many dog trainers say, there are no untrainable puppies; there are just untrained owners. So let's get you ready to teach your puppy like a professional!

How to Use This Book

The first section of this book will go over everything you need to know *before* your puppy comes home and starts training with you.

The second section will walk you through the first week of training with daily lessons and checklists. At the end is a graduation test that you can give your puppy at home!

Daily Lessons

Each lesson will teach you the cues, exercises, or manners to introduce to puppy that day.

Daily Checklists

The daily checklists outline how many cue, leash, or manners practices to have each day, and what to work on and for how long during each session.

You don't have to use these if you prefer to set up your training times in a different way. These checklists are simply meant as a general outline to follow if you feel overwhelmed and aren't sure what to practice when, or for how long.

If the number of training sessions listed is too much for you to fit into your daily schedule, don't stress! Puppy training is always easiest when both you and your dog are relaxed and having fun! As long as you practice everything your puppy has learned once a day, you should be fine. This might make it take longer than one week to complete everything in this booklet, but that's far better for your puppy than having rushed or stress-filled training sessions.

In the checklists we divide things in to several categories:

- General Cues
- Recall
- Leash Work
- House Manners
- Socialization

The General Cues are the majority of what your puppy will learn this week: Sit, Lay Down, Touch, Look, Leave It, Place, and Kennel Up.

Videos

Throughout this book you will find QR codes to training videos, like the code you saw at the end of the introduction. It looked like this:

If you haven't used a QR code before, all you have to do is pull out your phone, open its camera, and focus it on these codes. A tab will pop up on the screen asking if you want to open the link online. Tap on it, and it will take you to the training video for that section! It's as easy as that.

If you can't use QR codes with your phone, you can find the full playlist of exclusive training videos at this link:

PracticalPuppyTraining.com/week-one-videos

You will have to enter this password to view them: **MyPracticalPuppy!**

Have this playlist open on your computer or phone, and any time you come across a QR code in the booklet, watch the next video!

If you have any trouble accessing the videos, connect with me through my website, and we'll help figure out how to get you to them.

Happy training!

Training Prep

Puppy Personalities

Each puppy will respond to training differently based on their personality, and each will have different cues that they enjoy working on more than others. So don't be concerned if they pick up some things quickly but take more time to understand others.

Here are some general personalities/traits I often find in puppies I train. It is likely that yours will fall somewhere in one of these categories.

1. Fairly eager to please, usually confident and intelligent, and all puppy. They're more than willing to work with you, they typically have good food motivation, and they learn at a nice pace. Sometimes they get bored and want to play or take a nap instead. In the first few weeks of training they can get distracted by other sounds and movements in the area (which almost all puppies have a hard time ignoring at first!). Most puppies are in this category.

2. This puppy is willing to train, but is typically more easily distracted by things in his environment. Some distractions may be due to being slightly reactive to new sights and sounds. It can take them a day or two to warm up, but once they are comfortable they begin to blossom. Socialization is key to working with this kind of puppy. You'll need to provide great socialization and confidence building activities moving forward!

3. This puppy can be the most distracted, and is usually not food driven at all. They can be uninterested in working for treats, cheese, or even chicken. Some people might get frustrated and say they are difficult to train, but you just have to figure out what *does* motivate them to want to learn. Once you discover that, they become just as eager to please as any puppy! If your puppy is not food motivated, make sure to check out the Food Motivation section before starting training.

4. Very eager to please, and in most cases very intelligent. Some are food motivated, so they are willing to work for any kind of treat. They pick up on training quickly and easily. They love to think and figure out what it is you're asking them to do. This is the easiest pup to train, but if you don't keep on your toes, they could try to outsmart you and train *you* into doing what *they* want!

Training Theory

We use a "Positive Reinforcement" method to train puppies. That means we use two quadrants of learning theory, which we call **Positive Reinforcement** and **Removal Penalty**. Let's break that down.

- **Reinforcement** is anything that makes a behavior or action **more** likely to happen in the future.
- **Penalty** is anything that makes a behavior or action **less** likely to happen in the future.
- **Positive** means something is **added**, like a treat or toy.
- **Removal** means something is **removed**, like a bone, toy, or an open door being closed.

For example, if puppy rushes for the door when we open it, we would use **Removal Penalty** and close the door, removing the possibility of going outside. When the puppy reacts by doing something good like backing up or sitting nicely, we follow with **Positive Reinforcement**, marking the action with a "good job!" or "Yes!" and the door opening again so they can go outside.

"Removal Penalty" is meant to calmly—and without old-fashioned, aversive, or punishing techniques—help lead the dog into a behavior where Positive Reinforcement can be given. With the Positive Reinforcement method, you will never yell at, chase, or strike your dog—something which could cause incredible harm to their trust in you and to their training.

Basically, the Positive Reinforcement method we will be following is this:

Teach what you want.

Reinforce what you like.

Redirect what you don't.

The Structure of Training

Here's how you will teach your puppy to understand and follow through with Cues. You will want to be familiar with this by the time you get your pup and start training.

Pick a different cue word for each action, and make sure they aren't similar. A "Lay Down" for puppy to put their belly on the floor and a "Down" for them to get off of people would confuse them. Once your cue words are chosen, make sure everyone always uses the same word for the same action! Then you're ready to follow the structure of training: the Cue, Praise, and Reward.

Cue

Give the verbal or physical cue (Sit, Lay Down, etc.). And *don't give the cue again.* We want to teach puppy to respond on the first ask, not to wait for you to say Sit, Sit, Sit, SIT, and only respond when you use your "very serious or angry" voice. That would only teach your puppy to ignore you, and we don't want that!

Praise

As soon as your puppy performs the behavior you're looking for, mark it with a "Yes!" Puppy will quickly come to identify this word as praise for doing the right thing, and will eventually be happy with getting just this affirmation and not a treat.

If you are doing clicker training, the verbal praise of "Yes!" is replaced by a click.

When we train by marking correct actions with a sound or word like "Yes!", the mark must be given *at the moment* puppy offers the action you want, not several seconds later, and not before completing what they're supposed to do.

Reward

This is usually food or a treat, or sometimes a toy. It always comes at the end. You typically want to reward within 3 seconds of your praise.

So: Give the cue. Wait for puppy to complete the action. Praise with your marker word "Yes!" immediately. Then give your puppy a treat.

As training starts to advance, a release word will be introduced into the structure of training for some cues. I typically use "Free" or "Okay." This word will let your puppy know that they have completed the action you asked for and it is now okay to move. The release word happens after the praise of "Yes!" and either before or instead of the reward.

Play Video

Scan me!

When and What to Treat

When

During the first week of training, you're going to give your puppy a treat nearly every time they respond to a cue. You're teaching them that if they listen, good things happen.

We typically reward heavily with treats for the first 2-3 weeks of training. Once a cue becomes more established and they are responding immediately, we start to treat less often. We still

mark the good action with a "Yes!" and potentially some extra praise or a pet.

Starting to treat less often helps puppy begin to learn that they won't get a treat every time, which helps them to respond to cues even when you aren't holding food in the future.

When you start to treat less often, take it slow at first, skipping a treat once in every four to six cues. Approach it like a game. Puppy never knows how many cues he'll have to complete before he gets that next "payoff" of a treat.

what

Pick what your main treat will be during training sessions. Depending on the dog, I use kibble or soft puppy treats that can be broken in half. Use these during training sessions, then randomly give your puppy a different treat of varying value instead. If you mostly use soft treats, occasionally give them a piece of kibble, a tiny piece of cheese, or even a Cheerio or a piece of apple or banana!

Some dogs love certain fruits and veggies, while others will spit them out. Figure out what your dog likes, but make sure it is dog-friendly and not poisonous to them. Ex: Grapes and onions are harmful to dogs if consumed!

When you do this, especially once you start treating less often, your puppy never knows when or what the next treat could be. This keeps them guessing and highly engaged. They could get nothing, a piece of kibble, or they just might get a piece of cheese or turkey. That anticipation will keep them actively "playing the game" of training with you, and dogs love games!

Training Session Length

Once you know how to Cue, Praise, and Reward, the most important part of training is how long each session is. If it's too short, puppy won't learn anything. If it's too long, they'll become bored and frustrated, and will quickly come to dislike working with you. We never want that to happen!

The most important thing to remember is that puppies can only focus for about 1 minute per week of their age. If you start working with your dog at 8 weeks old, each training session can only be 8 minutes long. If your pup is 12 weeks old, no more than 12 minutes of training at a time.

A good formula is to have 3-5 short sessions a day. You can do one before each meal, and one or two in the middle of the day, or whatever works best for your schedule. Most puppies *can* complete this week of Bootcamp with just 2 sessions a day, but they *won't* be as well-practiced as they would be if you commit to 3-5 sessions a day.

Remember to make sure your puppy has plenty of time to nap and play between each training session!

As your dog gets older, you can start having 15-20 minute-long training sessions if you prefer. But I would recommend to never go over twenty minutes of focused work at a time while your dog is still a juvenile. It won't be fun for them anymore, they could get tired, and they will start trying to avoid being trained.

Just remember:

Try to have at least one training session for each meal you eat in a day, with one minute of work per week of age, and never more than 15-20 minutes at a time!

Your Training Space

For the first week of training, your puppy will be *very* easily distracted. They're not used to having to focus on one thing. Their brains are still developing!

To have productive training sessions, you're going to need a quiet space. Any sudden noises or movements, however small, can catch your puppy's attention. Then you will have to compete with this new thing to try to gain their attention again.

When you're going to have a training session, make sure your space and household is prepared. If you have little kids running around or if someone else walks past, puppy is going to want to chase them. Make sure your space is as quiet and still as possible.

Check and see what distractions might be on the floor. Pick up any toys, bones, or beds that your pup could decide they want to play with in the middle of training. Make yourself the most interesting thing in the   room and your training session will be smoother.

Play Video

Scan me!

Verbal and Physical Cues

Sometimes you might find yourself in a situation where it's not ideal to use a verbal cue with your dog. This is why we teach physical cues as well. The end goal is to have your dog respond to both the verbal and signed cue for any action, whether they're given simultaneously or separately. So if the physical cue for Sit is placing all five fingertips together pointed toward the sky, the dog would respond to either that hand cue by itself, saying "Sit!" without the hand cue, or the hand cue and "Sit!" together.

Lure or Offer

Every time you introduce a new cue to your puppy, they won't know what you're asking them to do. So, you have two options on how you can help them figure it out. Physical force, like pushing the puppy into a Sit or a Lay Down, is never the best way to teach them what you want; they're not thinking about what they're doing and choosing to do it. Instead of physical force, you can either Lure or let the pup Offer.

Lure

Luring a dog into the action you want is when you take a treat, let them sniff it, then move it in a way that when the dog follows your hand with their nose, they end up where you want them. This is usually a fast way to train a new cue, but it doesn't make the dog use their own brain as much as they could, which means the cue could take a little longer to become solidly ingrained.

Offer

When you let a pup offer the action on their own, you're letting them think through the problem you presented: "I want the treat,

but grabbing for it isn't working," and figure out for themselves what it is they have to do to get the treat out of your hand. This can take longer at the beginning than luring does, because your puppy has to think and process, but once they figure it out they are usually fast to respond, and proud of themselves!

You have to have patience when waiting for your puppy to Offer, especially when they're learning their first few cues. You usually end up sitting there with the treat in your hand while your pup tries to lick and paw to get it. Sometimes it can take a few minutes for them to give up trying to force the treat out of your hand and try something else, like sitting or lying down.

Play Video

Scan me!

The Practical Puppy

Yes and No

Your puppy will quickly learn the difference between the cues for "Yes" (that's good), and "No" (don't do that). This will naturally happen during training because you're going to use these cues a lot.

You already know the marker word "Yes!" When your pup hears this, they'll know they're doing something right and to do it again in the future.

The cue for "No" is "Ah-ah!" You say it loud, sharp, and quick. You can't say "ah-ah" in a soft or quiet way, because then puppy won't understand that it means "you're doing something bad and I want you to stop." The point is for this cue to sound very different from

"Yes!" which you want to say in a higher pitch, and with a smile or happy voice.

The "ah-ah" *has* to come across as firm. Many people with gentler personalities or softer voices have a hard time with this at first, but remember: it doesn't hurt your dog. It simply communicates to them in a way they understand.

Once your puppy knows these cues, you can use them anytime to mark behavior that you do or do not want, like a "Yes!" for them sitting at your feet instead of jumping on you, or an "Ah-ah!" if they grab a shoe to chew on.

There's a rule for Yes and No cues though. For every no you give your dog, you want to give them ten yeses. When you tell your puppy "No!" you're telling them what not to do… but not *what you want them to do instead*. So, they might stop the bad thing they're doing briefly, then go back to it, invoking another "Ah-ah!" from you.

If you catch your puppy doing something you don't want, tell them "Ah-ah!" and then guide them into something you *do* want them to do. Have them Sit. "Yes!" Lay Down. "Yes!" Have them chase a toy. "Yes!" Get on their bed. "Yes!" Then puppy will move away from the bad behavior and instead do things you do like and want, and they will hear more positive reinforcement instead of one "Ah-ah!" after another.

Shaping Work

Several cues that you will teach your puppy this week are built using Shaping Work. This means that the end goal of the cue is too complex to teach right from the beginning (example: having your dog leave a plate of chicken alone when it's sitting on the ground in front of them, or getting onto and staying on a dog bed until they've been released).

To reach the wanted end goal, these more complex cues are built over several weeks with Shaping Work. We have to slowly grow the cue in small steps. We always want puppy to succeed and understand what we're asking for, because then they'll be happy to keep learning. If we threw them into the final goal of these cues right away, we'd be setting them up for failure, and that would lead to frustration on both the human's and dog's sides.

In this first week of training we'll be introducing Stage One of cues like Leave It and Place, which can continue to become more impressive over time as a puppy progresses through the stages to the end goal.

Stress Behaviors

If a puppy is feeling stressed, overly pressured, or bored during their training sessions, they may exhibit behaviors like ignoring you, running away, or yawning. You'll need to know how to handle these situations if they arise.

The Bored Puppy

Here are some reasons why your puppy might be bored, and how to make them excited to train with you again:

1. If you drill one cue for too long, your dog will become sick of it. Switch things up and practice different cues for a while. See what your puppy is happiest to learn, and focus on that for a minute or two.

2. If your energy is low, your puppy might not respond as well as they could. Make sure your cues are firm but pleasant, and that your marker words and tone of voice when rewarding them are happy and approving. If your energy is higher, theirs will be as well.

3. Sometimes your puppy will just be tired. Let them have a break with enough time to nap or play, and come back to training later.

The Stressed Puppy

If your puppy runs away from you in the middle of a training session, it's likely that they're feeling too much pressure. Here are things to check for to alleviate their stress.

1. How long have you been training? If the session has gone on for too long, puppy will become over-worked, feel pressured, and want to run away.

2. How is your mood? If you sound annoyed or angry, your puppy will pick up on that. It will make them nervous and they will want to leave. Dogs like to please, so keep training positive!

3. Are you trying to push your puppy through training too fast and too soon? If you push a dog to learn faster than they are comfortable, they will feel the pressure, and that can lead to them bolting away from you. Relax your training sessions and let them learn at their own pace.

Food Motivation

Some puppies are more food motivated than others. The more food motivated a dog is, the easier they are to train, because they are happy to work for a "lesser" reward.

If your pup is food-driven, you can do most of your training with kibble or small, soft treats broken into pieces.

If your pup is not food-driven, you will usually find that out fast. They won't be interested in trying to figure out what you're teaching them. They might walk away from you, or try to crawl into your lap to cuddle instead of looking for the treat.

In this case you have three options.

1. You can use higher value rewards with your pup. Tiny pieces of chicken, turkey, cheese, etc. "Stinky" rewards like this can usually motivate even the least food-driven pup to learn. But sometimes a puppy isn't interested in any food rewards. In this case, option 2 or 3—or a mix of the two—is the way to go.

2. Regulate your puppy's meals. Feed them three times a day—a puppy's blood sugar can drop fast, so it's not safe to only feed them at morning and night. Have your training sessions before each meal, when your puppy is hungry and ready to eat, using pieces of their kibble as treats. Typically even the least food-driven dog is willing to work with you for their meals.

3. See what your puppy values over food. It could be pets, praise, or playing with a toy. If they love toys, try training them using those instead of treats. For example: If you're working on Sit, use the same marker word "Yes!" as soon as their rear touches the ground, then toss the toy down and play with them for a little while before taking it away and practicing the cue again. You can switch that out with pets or praise as well.

Socialization

Some people don't want to socialize their dogs until they've finished their first round of vaccines because they're worried that their puppy will pick up a disease from outside or off of other people.

We believe that the risk of having an unsocialized, scared, and flighty dog is far higher than the risk of them picking something up. And the reality is, anything they might have picked up out there will be brought back into your home on your clothes and the bottoms of your shoes anyway.

The prime time to socialize a dog and shape their confidence and behavior for the rest of their lives is between 7-16 weeks. Studies have shown that having as much positive neurological stimulation during this time period as possible is crucial to a puppy's development. So we start socialization right away.

With that in mind, do keep your pup away from any animal waste or garbage you see outside. Keep them away from other dogs you aren't familiar with, because you don't know if their owners have them up-to-date on their health care and vaccines. Try to avoid high dog-traffic areas.

I also recommend not taking young puppies to dog parks for two reasons. With so many dogs off-leash it would be easy for one of them to come up on your puppy, intimidating him before he was comfortable enough to say hello on his own terms. If your puppy gets scared like this, it could make him warry of unknown dogs in the future. While your puppy is in his prime socialization weeks, you want every experience he has with other dogs to be a good one.

Two, there is the risk of an aggressive dog attacking another dog in the park. I personally have heard too many horror stories to be comfortable taking puppies to dog parks.

If you decide to keep your puppy in your home until they've had all their vaccines, make sure to start socializing them well by doing what you can within your house. We'll have both "Out & About" and "At Home" socialization sections in the daily training segments below.

Training: Week One

The End Goals

Your puppy is going to learn a lot this week! Here are the things you'll work on and what the end goal is for Day 7.

This might sound overwhelming, but puppies pick up on it fast. It will be easier than you think—all it takes is a little time and patience!

- **SIT** — *The goal: To get your puppy to the point where sit is becoming automatic.*
- **LAY DOWN** — *The goal: To lay down on cue.*
- **WALKING ON THE LEASH** — *The goal: For puppy to be comfortable with the leash and start walking alongside you.*
- **PLACE – STAGE I** — *The goal: For puppy to get on their mat and sit when cued, staying for 1 minute.*
- **LEAVE IT – STAGE I** — *The goal: For puppy to wait and not attempt to take treats from either palm when both are held out on either side of his nose.*
- **LOOK – STAGE I** — *The goal: For puppy to choose to make eye contact with you when cued.*
- **TOUCH** — *The goal: For puppy to touch your hand with their nose when cued.*

- **RECALL EXERCISES** — *The goal: To have puppy choose to run to you when called from a lead or short distance.*
- **FOOD MANNERS** — *The goal: For puppy to sit and wait to be fed, not jumping up or diving into the bowl before you set it down.*
- **CRATE TRAINING** — *The goal: For puppy to understand that the cue "Kennel Up!" means to go in the crate, and for them to start sleeping through the night.*
- **POTTY TRAINING** — *The goal: For them to start to understand that they shouldn't go potty inside, and to increase the time they can hold it while running loose to at least 30-45 minutes.*
- **GROOMING** — *The goal: To introduce puppy to brushes and grooming tools and have him comfortable with them touching him.*
- **SOCIALIZATION** — *The goal: For puppy to be comfortable going on walks, short drives, exploring and walking on new things, and meeting "new" people or dogs.*

Day One

It's day one, and if you just brought your puppy home they have a lot of changes happening in life. We're going to keep it pretty simple today. We'll ease them into training by starting with just one cue and introducing them to normal household life.

The goals today are to get them acquainted with the leash and crate, start potty training, and to learn to Sit.

Your puppy might try to climb into your lap during training sessions at first. They don't understand that you have tasty treats and are trying to teach them something. Give them a treat so they know what you have. Then try to block them from climbing into your lap, or if they're already there, gently move them back to the floor and redirect their attention to training. You can give them lots of snuggles when the training session is over!

Sit

The first thing we always teach our puppies is to Sit. This simple cue is a great way to help shape calm behavior in the future. It can be used in many everyday inter-actions with your dog.

While the verbal cue for Sit is "Sit," the hand cue we use is placing all five fingers together and pointing them toward the ceiling.

Since puppy doesn't know what any cues mean yet, (or even that we're trying to teach them something!) we'll be slightly changing our structure of training, the **Cue, Praise, and Reward**.

The first few times we have puppy Sit, don't say the cue word at all. It would just add more noise and confusion to the situation for them. Hold out the treat and let

Play Video

Scan me!

The Practical Puppy

them smell it. Don't let them have it. Wait patiently until their rear touches the ground. It might take a minute or two, and they will try to get the treat out of your hand.

Remember, they don't know you're trying to teach them something. Wait. Give them time to think it over and figure out what it is they have to do to be given the treat.

Remember, they don't know you're trying to teach them something. Wait. Give them time to think it over and figure out what it is they have to do to be given the treat.

As *soon* as their back end touches the floor, give the marker word of "Yes!" and let them have the treat.

Repeat. Once your puppy has put his bottom on the ground a few times and is starting to understand what he needs to do to get the treat, you can introduce the cue word and hand signal.

Say "Sit!" when you hold out the treat and form the hand signal. Wait for their bottom to touch the ground, then give the marker word "Yes!" and reward with the treat.

Puppies usually pick up on Sit pretty quickly. Sometimes it only takes one training session. But don't worry if you have to work on it a few times today before they start to understand.

This is their first training session ever, so don't make them work on it for too long at a time! Stop after 4-7 minutes, and try to end on a good note (them placing their rear on the ground fairly quickly after you give the cue word).

Leash Work

Since your puppy has probably never had a leash on before, don't start by going for a walk right away. They would likely pull and buck against it, and we want to avoid that. For the first week the most important thing to remember is to *never pull on the leash.*

On day one, clip the leash on your puppy's collar and just let them drag it around. You can do this inside, out in

your yard, or even in a park if you are far away from any roads and there aren't other people or animals around that could be unsafe.

Let them drag the leash around 3-4 times today. Since they don't have to mentally focus on this, you can let them drag it for 10-20 minutes each time. Let them follow you around the house or chase you in your yard.

Don't leave the leash on your puppy if you aren't supervising them though. You don't want them to get stuck on something or start chewing on it!

This exercise will help them become comfortable with the leash hanging from their collar and feeling slight pressure as they drag it around.

Crate Training

During the day

If you introduce your puppy to the crate before they have to sleep in it overnight, it will make crate training easier for both you and them. Bring puppy over to the crate and leave the door open. Show them a treat, then toss

it inside and say "Kennel Up!" Once puppy goes in to get it, mark the action with "Yes!" and wait for them to come back out. Do this several times, until they're happy to "play the game" with you.

Now, do the same thing, but once they're inside and you've marked it with "Yes!" close the door. Once they see that they're

stuck inside, they might scratch at the door or bark. Wait until they do not push at the door or make noise for 5 seconds. As soon as they're calm for those five seconds, mark it with "Yes!", immediately open the door, and give them a treat.

Now you can mix these two up so puppy never knows if they'll be able to come out of the crate right away, or if they have to stay in it for a few seconds. This will help them understand that going into the crate is okay and they won't always be locked inside of it.

Play Video

Scan me!

During the rest of the day, leave the crate open so they can go inside if they choose to. Have a blanket or toy in there. Occasionally throw a treat inside it for puppy to find the next time they explore the crate on their own.

The goal is to help this become your puppy's "safe place." Make sure that if you ever find puppy resting in their crate, you leave them alone. Don't reach inside to pet them or pull them out. Think of it as your puppy's room. If they go there they are likely tired or are saying they need some space. If you don't let them have it, they will stop using it.

At night

Most 8 week old puppies can go to sleep around 10 at night and make it without a potty break until around 5:30 in the morning. It depends on each puppy and how long they can hold their bladder though. Usually they will only have a few random accidents in their crate overnight before they figure it out. They don't want their sleeping space to be messy!

To help them last overnight, remove their access to food and water by 7 p.m.

When it's time to go to bed, take your pup to the crate, say "Kennel Up", put them in, and give them a treat. Close the door and walk away. They will probably cry for at least the first few nights. Ignore them, and they'll go to sleep eventually. Make sure the crate is in a fairly dark and quiet place. If they hear people moving around, they will likely keep crying.

Some puppies will be quiet until the early morning when they have to go potty. When you hear them start crying, get up and take them outside right away. They will pee and likely poo within the first 5 minutes of being outside the crate.

Other puppies will cry in the middle of the night. If they've only been in the crate for a few hours, they're probably fine. If it's 3 or 4 in the morning, they might have to go pee. Take them outside, but don't talk to them or play with them. If they don't pee quickly once you set them down, put them back to bed. Don't make a big deal about it. Place them in the crate quietly and walk away.

If your puppy has to go potty in the early morning, don't let them sleep on the bed with you when you bring them back inside, even if it's just for an hour or two. If you do, they will quickly learn that if they cry at 3 or 4 a.m., you will let them be on the bed for the rest of the night. It will become their routine. They will cry at 3 a.m. every night.

Occasionally, there will be a loud puppy that won't stop crying when you put them to bed. They are either vocal by nature or they are just scared to be alone and are nervous in this new situation. If it's been 15 minutes since you put them to bed and they are still crying, or they cry all through the night, there are a few things you can try.

Place the crate next to your bed. A lot of puppies will be quiet if they're in the same room as someone. If that doesn't work, for the first night or two you can place the crate on your bed with your hand near the door.

Once they start to sleep better, each night you can move the crate further away from the bed, then eventually out of your room and toward wherever you want the dog to sleep long-term.

Potty Training

Some puppies will pick up on this quickly, others will take some time. If you set a schedule and stick to it, you shouldn't have too many accidents in your home. Remember to always supervise your puppy if they are loose in your house. The more accidents they have, the more they think it's okay to go potty inside.

Set up a small exercise pen to aid in potty training. It will be invaluable to the process—dogs don't like to use their living space as a bathroom. Being in the smaller space of an exercise pen will help your puppy slowly learn to hold their bladder.

Start by taking your puppy potty outside. Once they've gone they can come inside for supervised play time.

If you bring your puppy home at 8 weeks of age, take them out every 20 minutes while they are free. You will quickly find out if your pup immediately squats each time, or if they just run around and play, which means they can hold it longer.

Once they've had a play time for 20-40 minutes, put them in the exercise pen. Leave them there for 1 hour or until they wake up from their nap. Then immediately take them out to go potty before they have another supervised play time.

If you keep your puppy on this schedule during the day, and always watch them when they are loose, you shouldn't have many accidents in your home.

Over this first week, your puppy's bladder control should slowly grow until they need a potty break about every 40 minutes when they're awake and loose with you.

Every pup has different bladder control, so some will have to go all the time at first, and others will be able to hold it for 30-40 minutes right away.

So:

Take them out every 20 minutes when loose. Once they don't squat within 2-3 minutes of being outside, increase the time. Take them out every 25 minutes until they don't squat right away. Then take them out every 30 minutes, etc.

Day One Checklist

SESSION 1:

Cues
Work on Sit for 4-7 minutes.

Leash Work
Let puppy drag their leash for 10-20 minutes.

SESSION 2:

Cues
Work on Sit and Kennel Up for 8 minutes.

Leash Work
Let puppy drag their leash for 10-20 minutes.

SESSION 3:

Cues
Work on Sit and Kennel Up for 8 minutes.

Day Two

Your puppy should understand that you're trying to teach him things now, which means he'll be more willing to focus and try to figure out what you want him to do. Today we'll be adding in three new cues.

Leash Work

Once it looks like they're comfortable with the leash and not paying attention to it while dragging it around, you can start to play the Drag & Grab game.

Drag & Grab

While your puppy is dragging their leash, walk alongside them and grab the end of the leash. Hold it loosely or just draped over two of your fingers. If puppy stops, goes in a different direction, or does anything that pulls against the leash, let it slip out of your hand. For now, *never pull on the leash.*

The Practical Puppy

You're teaching puppy that the leash is not scary, and pulling on it would *make* it scary, because they've probably never had pressure applied to their collar before.

Anytime you come alongside them and pick up the leash, praise them with "good job!" or "Yes!" while they walk near you without pulling on it. As soon as there's pressure, let the leash drop, wait a moment, then go try again.

They will slowly start to understand that the leash isn't a bad thing, and that when you hold it, it's good for them to stay near you.

Once they're used to the leash and not pulling against it all the time, you can start going for walks, but for this week, practice leash walking like this when you can.

If you're going for a walk outside where you can't safely drop the leash and your puppy stops or pulls back against it, drop to one knee, spread your arms out to your sides, and call them excitedly. Most puppies

will respond to this, especially if they stopped because the pressure on their leash made them nervous. This is still very new to them. When they come to you, give them a quick pet, stand, say "Let's Go" or "Heel," and continue walking.

Play Video

Scan me!

If that doesn't work, play the Pressure & Release game.

Pressure & Release

Give a small tug on the line with a gentle, consistent pressure. As *soon* as they move towards you release the pressure and say "Yes!"

Play Video

Scan me!

To get them to repeat the good action (moving toward you), you have to mark it with the release of pressure the moment it happens—don't drag them all the way to you. If they stop before they get to you, repeat the Pressure & Release.

Your first walks will likely be very stop-and-start, but that's OK. Just remember to never drag your puppy forward!

Leave It

Leave It is built using Shaping Work. This week we're working on Stage One.

The cardinal rule for working on the Leave It cue is that *the treat must always come from your hand.* While working this cue, never

Play Video

[QR code]

📱Scan me!

let the puppy take a treat from the ground or from a hand he is currently trying to get it from.

Put a piece of treat in both of your hands. Hold them out, palms open, on either side of your puppy's nose. You might have to show them to him so he knows you have something. When he goes to grab one, close your hand over the treat and say "Leave It." When he gives up and goes for the treat in your other hand, close that one, open the first one, and say "Leave It."

Once puppy has gone from one hand to the other 2-4 times, say "Take It!" and let them have one of the treats. Vary how many times they have to "bounce" between your hands before they get the reward, but never make them go back and forth more than 4 times in one Leave It.

It can take puppies several times to start to understand that they can't get the treat by grabbing for it. They might focus on one hand, ignoring the other. If this happens, slowly move your closed hand back and your open hand over to take its spot. When their nose moves towards your open hand, close it and say "Leave It" again. Eventually they'll figure out that this cue means there are two treats, one in each hand, and they will start to "bounce" their nose between your hands, waiting to see which one will give them the treat.

If your puppy ever pulls back, sits, or makes any backward movement away from your hands and the treats, immediately mark it with a "Yes!" and give them one of the treats.

The end goal for the first stage of Leave It is for puppy to "bounce" their nose in-between your hands without trying to grab the treats, or if they progress quickly, to sit back and just look at your hands, waiting for you to offer them a treat.

Place

The cue for Place, "go there and stay there" also builds over several weeks with Shaping Work. This means that the end goal—your dog going to their bed when asked and staying there calmly until they're released—is too complicated to teach right away. We have to slowly build the cue toward the end goal in small steps.

For now it's best to use something that your dog will only see while working on Place. So pick a bed or towel and keep it put away unless you're working on the cue.

Anytime you work on place, *always reward by tossing the treat onto the mat, not by giving it to them from your hand.* We want them to see the mat as a happy place that gives them lots of tasty things if they stay on it. We want their focus to be more on the mat than on us.

The first step is to reward your puppy anytime they show interest in their mat, bed, or towel. Set the mat down, then wait for puppy to either sniff it or step on it. Mark that action with a "Yes!" and drop a treat onto the bed. If they don't see it, point it out to them.

Wait for puppy to run off the mat, and once they go back to sniff or step on it, repeat the marker and reward. After a few times you can start saying "Place!" and pointing to the mat. Reward as soon as they sniff or step on it.

If your pup sits or stays on the mat for more than a few seconds, mark and reward again so they know that remaining on the mat is a good thing.

Play Video

Scan me!

Look

Look is a difficult cue for dogs. They don't like maintaining eye contact since they typically see it as confrontation or aggression. So, just like Leave It and Place, Look is built in several steps, growing your dog's comfort level and trust. This week we just want puppy to learn to glance up and meet your eyes on cue. They can look away right away. We can teach them to hold the eye contact later.

Only start to teach Look after your puppy knows what treats are and is willing to work for them, and only "drill" the cue 4-5 times in a row. Since this one is harder for your puppy to do, we don't want to wear them out. After 4-5 times, take a break or practice something else for a minute before going back to asking for a Look.

Show your puppy a small treat, then toss it out a short way from you. Wait for them to grab it. Then you're going to wait until they look up and make eye contact with you. This could take a while. Puppy is going to sniff around, lick your hands, and maybe try to crawl into your lap. They're trying to figure out how to get another treat. Eventually they will look up at you to see why you're sitting

The Practical Puppy

so still. As soon as they meet your eyes, say "Yes!" and toss another treat out a short distance.

Repeat.

Once they seem to understand that they're supposed to look up at you, you can add the verbal cue "Look!" but wait to say it until they're done eating the treat you just tossed out! And remember, only give the verbal cue once. We don't want them to learn to ignore your cues. If they don't respond, just wait silently until they do.

Play Video

[] Scan me!

Socialization

What to know before you get started:

Every puppy will have a different confidence level, so socialize them at their own speed.

If yours is happy and waggily on walks and with meeting new people, you could probably take them into a small hardware store with you later this week. If your puppy hunkers down during walks, doesn't like seeing other people, and gets scared at cars passing by, you probably want to stick with walks for a little while and not overwhelm them with going to even more new places.

If you're on a walk, and something scares them and they cower—stop. Don't force them to move toward the scary thing, but don't let them run away either. Make sure you seem confident and reassure them with your voice. If need be, you can bend down to pet them, but again, make sure you are confident. If you seem nervous or reassure them too dramatically, they will assume that there *is* something to be afraid of. Wait until puppy offers to move forward or toward you by himself, and praise! Walk around the scary thing if you have to, but don't "run away" from it with your puppy.

If/when you introduce puppy to "new" people that don't live in your house this week, make sure it's a positive, happy experience. If someone is ever overwhelming puppy, chasing them, or if a child is hurting them, remove the dog or the person from the situation immediately.

If/when you introduce your puppy to other dogs this week, take it slow. If you put your puppy out in a yard with five of your friend's dogs, they would likely feel overwhelmed, intimidated, or scared. And that experience could influence your pup to always be nervous when they see an unknown dog in the future.

Instead, introduce them to "new" dogs one at a time, and keep them both on leashes at first. That way the other dog can't overwhelm your puppy by getting in their space and saying too enthusiastic of a "Hi!" before your puppy is ready. This will help them be more comfortable, which will build their confidence, rather than their fear, in meeting other animals.

Today:

Start socialization today by taking puppy for walks around your neighborhood or nearby park. Passing other people, seeing other dogs across the street, cars driving by, hearing people play basketball, or seeing kids on bikes—these are all great things to introduce and will start getting puppy comfortable with the world.

Day Two Checklist

SESSION 1:

Cues
Work on Sit and Leave It for 8 minutes.

Leash Work
Let puppy drag their leash for 10-20 minutes, randomly picking up the leash to walk with them.

SESSION 2:

Cues
Work on Place for 3 minutes. For 5 minutes, introduce Look, working on Sit and Leave It in between asking for Looks.

Leash Work
Go for a short walk outside, calling puppy to you or playing the Pressure & Release game if they pull against the leash.

SESSION 3:

Cues
Work on Place for 2 minutes, then Sit, Look, and Leave It for 6 minutes.

SESSION 4:

Cues
Work on Place for 2 minutes, then Kennel Up, Look, Leave It, and Sit for 6 minutes.

Day Three

Today we're going to start learning three new cues. After this, your puppy will be introduced to most of the cues they'll be practicing this week!

Lay Down

Show your dog the treat in your hand, then hold it next to the floor and don't say anything. Wait while they try to get the treat from you. Eventually he'll end up laying down. As soon as this happens, give the "Yes!" marker and let him have the treat. Just like with Sit, do this a few times before adding in the verbal cue "Lay Down."

Once they start to understand what "Lay Down" means, add in the physical

Play Video

Scan me!

cue. Hold your hand out flat and swipe it down. Do this while saying "Lay Down!" and end with your hand resting against the floor, holding the treat there. As soon as puppy follows your hand and lies down, reward with the "Yes!" and treat.

Touch

This is an easy cue for puppy to learn, since they see it as a game! "Touch" is a nose targeting cue that can be used to teach many other tricks in the future. By itself, it can be helpful when your dog is already in close proximity to you but you need them to move somewhere else. You can also use it in the future to help teach Nice Greetings (not jumping up on people).

Start by holding your hand an inch from their nose. Say "Touch!" and wait until they bop your fingers with their nose. They might try to paw your hand, but ignore it and wait until their nose touches you. Mark it with a "Yes!" and give them a treat. Do this a couple times over, moving your hand to a new place each time, but keeping it in very close proximity to them.

Play Video

📱Scan me!

Recall

We build up consistent recall very slowly. The main thing to remember in the beginning is to NEVER cue a recall unless you know puppy will follow through with it. Every time someone cues a recall and puppy *doesn't* come, it sets recall training back, and puppy quickly learns that they don't have to follow through if they don't want to.

They will start to ignore you.

For this reason I use the verbal cue "Here!" instead of "Come!" with some dogs. It's too easy for someone to call for a dog to "come!" without thinking about it, or in instances where the untrained dog is never going to come; if they're chasing a squirrel, if they're running toward someone new to say Hi, or even if they've just found a very interesting smell to follow. Choose which cue word is best for you to use and stick with it.

You never want to chase your dog after cueing a recall. If you do, they will think it is a game, and games are a good thing. They will learn that a recall cue means they should run away and play the game with you.

If a cue happens, they don't respond, and they're not on a line where you can "reel" them in to you, you have two options.

1. Run or back AWAY from them while sounding excited. It is hard for a pup to resist their chase instinct.
2. Bend down on one knee, spreading your arms out to your sides, and say their name excitedly. A dog will respond to this posture nearly every time.

You also never want to discipline, chastise, or be angry at your dog after they respond to a recall and come to you. Even if they were

being naughty a few seconds ago, the last thing they remember doing is listening to you and coming when called. If you discipline them for that, you're teaching them it's a bad thing to do what you ask, and they will very quickly stop responding to any recalls.

For the first week, only cue a recall when your puppy is on a leash or a short line, or if they're already running towards you. This way if they don't respond you can slowly draw them to you in excitement and fun.

Play Video

Scan me!

When your puppy is on the leash, move backwards and say your cue word. Again, sounding excited and moving away from them is key. As soon as they are running up to you say "Yes!" Give them a treat when they reach you.

With recall, you always want to make it a party anytime they come to you. If coming to you means excitement, fun, and attention, they are going to want to respond.

If they're on the leash or line and don't respond to your cue for "Here," play the Pressure & Release game.

Give a small tug on the line. As *soon* as they move towards you release the pressure and say "Yes!"

To get them to repeat the good action (moving toward you), you have to mark it by releasing the pressure the moment they take that first step—don't drag them all the way to you. If they stop before they get to you, repeat the Pressure & Release.

Socialization

Out & About:

If your puppy seems fairly confident on walks now and isn't cowering or acting scared, take them for a brief

drive in the car today. If you want to take your dog with you places in the future, or just have them comfortable being driven to the groomers and vet, now is the best time to start getting them accustomed to car rides. If you can, take them somewhere they can get out and play each time, or give them treats in the crate. You want to make the experience fun!

At Home:

There are many things you can do within your home to help socialize your dog and grow their confidence. The daily sights and sounds of life at home are a great start. Let them see you use brooms, vacuums, and mops. Make some noise in the kitchen with your pots and pans. With any of these, if puppy seems curious, comes closer, or doesn't run away, say "Yes!" and give them a treat. This helps them learn not to react in fear to new things or loud and unexpected noises. Always encourage, and if they are brave enough to explore the new or noisy thing, mark and reward!

Day Three Checklist

SESSION 1:

Cues
Work on Sit, Leave It, Look, and Touch for 8 minutes.

Leash Work
Let puppy drag their leash for 10-20 minutes, randomly picking up the leash to walk with them. Try going for a short walk outside.

SESSION 2:

Cues
Work on Place for 3 minutes. Practice Sit and introduce Lay Down for 5 minutes.

Leash Work
Try going for a short walk outside.

SESSION 3:

Cues
Practice Recall on a leash or short line for 3 minutes. Work on Sit, Lay Down, and Touch for 5 minutes.

SESSION 4:

Cues
Work on Place for 2 minutes, practice Recall for 2 minutes, then work on Kennel Up, Look, and Leave It for 4 minutes.

Socialization:
Take puppy for a short car ride. Let them see you use a vacuum, mop, or noisy pots and pans.

Day Four

For the next two days, we won't introduce any new cues to your puppy. Practice everything they've learned so far. We want to grow their confidence in these cues, helping their reactions become faster and more ingrained in their memory.

Place

If your puppy is now automatically stepping on their mat or bed when you cue for a "Place," still say "Yes!" right away, but wait to drop a treat on the mat until they Sit on it. As soon as their rear touches the mat, mark the action with another "Yes!" and toss them a treat.

If they seem confused and don't Sit, help them by cueing for a Sit while they are standing on the mat, then mark it with a "Yes!" and drop the treat in front of them.

From now on, verbally mark the action of getting on the mat with a "yes!" but don't reward with a treat until they are sitting on it.

Once they are sitting on the mat, see if they will stay there for a short time. If they do, reward with another "Yes!" and

Play Video

Scan me!

treat. For now, reward often if they stay on the mat—every 5-20 seconds that they remain in place. Don't expect them to stay for too long yet. Even just thirty seconds is great!

Leash Work

Your puppy should now be very used to having the leash attached to his collar and to having you hold it. Still play the Drag & Grab game when you can, but start going for more "real" walks now.

If your puppy walks too slowly or stops, play the Pressure & Release game. Don't drag them.

If they move too fast and walk in front of you, putting pressure on the line, you're going to play the Stop & Go game.

Stop & Go

Anytime your pup pulls on the lead, stop. Wait in place until they back up or release that pressure against the lead. As soon as there is slack, say "Yes!" and move forward again.

Sit to Get

Now that puppy knows Sit pretty well, you can start using this to shape calm behavior and nice manners. Think of Sit as the way your puppy says please. Your puppy wants the new toy in your hand? They have to say please. They want pets? Say please. Anything that your puppy wants from you, whether it's an object, food, or attention, have them Sit first.

You can use this "Sit to say Please!" tool to teach many things in the future, including Food and Door Manners!

Socialization

At Home:

Start getting your puppy used to seeing people in all sorts of clothes, including hats and canes! We've seen adult dogs that are fully confident in most situations become scared and run away at seeing someone in a baseball cap for the first time.

Out & About:

It's also important for your puppy to be seeing all sorts of people. If your puppy is adjusting well to your home and is no longer show-ing signs of worry, have them meet family members or friends who look different from you! If a puppy is never exposed to children, men with beards, someone in a wheelchair, etc., they could show fear when they encounter these people as an adult.

Day Four Checklist

SESSION 1:

Cues
Work on Sit, Lay Down, Leave It, Look, and Touch for
8 minutes.

Leash Work
Go for a short walk outside.

SESSION 2:

Cues
Work on Place for 3 minutes. Work on general cues for
5 minutes.

Leash Work
Go for a short walk outside.

SESSION 3:

Cues
Practice Recall on a leash or short line for 3 minutes. Work
on general cues for 5 minutes.

SESSION 4:

Cues
Work on Place for 2 minutes, practice Recall for 2 minutes,
then work on general cues for 4 minutes.

Socialization
Put on a fashion show for your puppy! Let them see you
in hats, different shoes, or clothes that look different than
what they've seen before.
Introduce puppy to 2 "new" people who look
different from you.

Day Five

Touch

Start to move your hand a few inches further away from your puppy when you ask for a touch. See if they will get up and take a step or two to reach your hand. If they don't, do a Touch with your hand an inch from their nose again, then slowly increase the distance you ask them to move their nose to complete a Touch until they have to take a step to reach it.

Place

Slowly increase the time puppy stays on the mat. Have them sit, and reward often if they stay there. They should figure out that remaining on the mat is good and begin to stay there for longer periods of time before running off of it. Keep rewarding for every 5-30 seconds they stay on the mat, and see if they will start to stay for 30-60 seconds total.

Add in the release cue word, "Free!" or "Okay!" to call them off the mat. For now, if they step off by themselves say the release cue immediately. After a moment, point to the mat and say "Place!" again.

Remember to only work on Place for a few minutes at a time so your puppy doesn't get frustrated and give up!

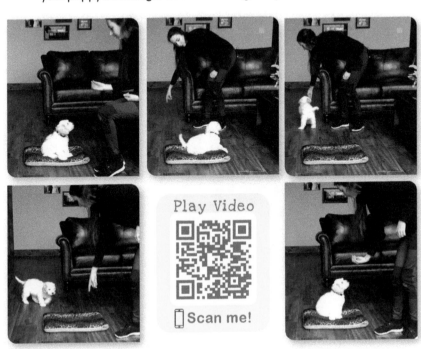

Play Video

Scan me!

Socialization

Out & About:

If your puppy seems fairly
confident and comfortable
while out on walks, try taking them to a pet or hardware store today! Pick a
place that is smaller or
quieter. You don't want to
overwhelm puppy. If you
get in the store and they

freeze up, wait a moment and offer them some encouragement.
If they perk up and are comfortable following you, let them walk
around and explore. Stop anytime they do and let them sniff or
watch people moving around.

If they show fear, give them verbal encouragement. Some puppies could end up overwhelmed and not want to walk by themselves at all. Pick them up and carry them, still offering calm verbal

encouragement. Don't stay in the store for too long, and when you get back to the car or your home offer them treats and lots of praise! The first time or two in a public place can intimidate puppies. Let them take it at their own pace, and they will quickly adapt and start to have fun on their outings!

At Home:

Place something on the ground that they've never seen before or has a "scary" shape or sound, like a paper bag, bottles, or even a basketball. When they explore it, mark and reward with a "Yes!" and a treat.

Get them used to walking on all sorts of materials. Having something that feels different, or even moves, beneath the paws can scare dogs if they aren't exposed to similar things as a puppy.

If you have a plastic puppy exercise pen, lay one panel flat on the ground and lure your puppy over it with a treat. They might not like the feel of the plastic underneath their paws. If they seem worried, upgrade to a higher reward treat, like cheese or chicken. You can do the same thing with a piece of cardboard, crinkly paper, pieces of wood, etc.

Day Five Checklist

SESSION 1:

Cues
Work on Sit, Lay Down, Leave It, Look, and Touch for 8 minutes.

Leash Work
Go for a short walk outside.

SESSION 2:

Cues
Work on Place for 3 minutes. Work on general cues for 5 minutes.

Leash Work
Go for a short walk outside.

SESSION 3:

Cues
Practice Recall on a leash or short line for 3 minutes. Work on general cues for 5 minutes.

SESSION 4:

Cues
Work on Place for 2 minutes, practice Recall for 2 minutes, then work on general cues for 4 minutes.

Socialization
Take puppy for a short car ride to a small pet or hardware store.

Have puppy explore two "scary" objects (paper bag, basketball, etc.) and walk over two surfaces that they aren't used to feeling under their paws (cookie sheets, cooling racks, bubble wrap, etc.).

Day Six

Since your puppy has a nice Sit now, we're going to introduce Food Manners today. This will start nice house manners and will help your pup learn to be a little more calm and respectful within your home and around your family.

Lay Down

Once puppy is responding to Lay Down well, you can start trying to cue for it while standing in front of them instead of sitting on the floor with them. They will likely be confused at first. Your position has changed so they think the cue must have as well. Cue for the Lay Down while standing up. If they don't follow through, bend over

Play Video

Scan me!

to give them the cue with your hand ending next to the floor. They should respond. Eventually they should start to understand that the Lay Down cue is the same while you are standing.

Food Manners

Now that your puppy knows Sit well, you can teach them to have nice manners when they're fed. At meal time, fill their bowl and let them know it has food in it. Go to where you want to feed them. They will probably jump or wiggle around. Tell them to Sit.

As soon as their rear touches the ground, say "Yes!" and I
to set the food bowl down. If they lunge for it or stand, straig.... ....
back up and try again. The first few times it will be hard for puppy
to wait while the food bowl is being lowered, so don't lower it
too slowly—remember, we want to set them up for success. A
puppy won't be able to wait long when food manners are still so
new to them.

Play Video

Scan me!

Socialization

Out & About:

See if you can find something new for your puppy to observe while out on a walk today. This could be people playing in a basketball court, someone on a bike, scooter, or skateboard, a jogger, etc. Let puppy observe from a distance. Don't make them get closer if they don't want to. If you don't see anyone while on a walk, get someone from your family to help you out by biking or jogging past you and puppy a few times!

At Home:

Set up a tunnel for your puppy to go through. If you don't have a dog or kitten tunnel, create one with chairs and blankets! Toss treats inside that your puppy has to go find. This helps them learn to be calm and confident even when moving through darker or smaller spaces.

Day Six Checklist

Food Manners
Work on Food Manners at feeding times.

Cues
Work on Sit, Lay Down, Leave It, Look, and Touch for
8 minutes.

Leash Work
Go for a walk outside.

Cues
Work on Place for 4 minutes and Recall for 4 minutes.

Leash Work
Go for a walk outside.

Cues
Practice Recall on a leash or short line for 3 minutes. Work
on general cues for 5 minutes.

Cues
Work on Place for 4 minutes, then work on general cues
for 4 minutes.

Socialization
Let puppy observe new-to-them outdoor activities like
bikers or joggers.

Set up a tunnel and encourage them to walk through.

Introduce puppy to 2 "new" people today and one
"new" dog.

Day Seven

Today is the last day of Puppy Bootcamp Week One! Keep practicing cues and manners—the graduation test comes after this!

Touch

Continue to ask for Touch with your hand further away from your puppy. See if they will complete a touch where they have to take 4-6 steps to reach your hand with their nose.

Place

Continue to reward often when your pup is sitting and staying on their mat. See if they will stay there for 1-1 ½ minutes before you release them with "Free!" or "Okay!", or they try to move off of it on their own.

Grooming

Although your pup's coat is likely short enough that they don't need to be groomed yet, this is the best time to start getting them used to brushes, scissors, and nail clippers. This will make both your and your groomer's life easier in the future, and help your dog learn to be calm and confident in these situations.

Let your puppy inspect any new brushes or scissors, but don't let them chew on them! Before you set the brush against their fur, you can brush another dog or even your own arm so they can see that it's not scary.

When you brush your pup, never start by bringing the brush down over their head. They can't see it there, and it can make them feel like they're being attacked. Start by brushing the sides in slow strokes. Fast or harsh strokes can also make your pup feel attacked, so keep it slow and gentle.

Let them sniff it in between brush strokes if they want. If they really don't like it, wait 10 seconds between brushings, praise them when you brush, or even give them a chewy treat or bone to focus on instead. Slowly move on to brushing their back, ears, head, tail, and feet. The head, tail, and paws can be extra sensitive, so be gentle!

The Practical Puppy

If you have hair scissors, keep them closed and touch them along your pup's body, around their paws, on their ears, and between their eyes. This is important for dogs with long-haired coats because they're going to be trimmed all the time in the future!

Play Video

Scan me!

With nail clippers, just let puppy see them and hear you open and close them, moving them closer to their feet. Praise and reward. When it is time to clip their nails, take it slow if they don't like it. Give them a 10 second break between every nail or two, and praise as you make each trim. It's important that you are calm and confident, because if your pup senses that you're worried, they're going to be worried too.

Socialization

At Home:

This is the Prize Box Game! Set up a box or basket of odds and ends, like glass bottles that clink, empty plastic water bottles that crinkle, some dog toys, balled up newspaper—get creative! Hide a few high-prize treats like chicken or cheese in the basket. Your puppy will have to explore the box to find the treats. He'll have to move things around, which means they'll make noise and bump against him. This game helps teach puppies to be calm and confident while unexpected things happen around them.

Day Seven Checklist

SESSION 1:

Cues
Work on Sit, Lay Down, Leave It, Look, and Touch for
8 minutes.

Leash Work
Go for a walk outside.

SESSION 2:

Cues
Work on Place for 4 minutes. Work on Recall for 4 minutes.

Leash Work
Go for a walk outside.

SESSION 3:

Cues
Work on Sit, Lay Down, Leave It, Look, and Touch for
8 minutes.

Grooming
Introduce puppy to grooming tools and being brushed.

Socialization
Take puppy for a short car ride.

Play the prize box game.

Congratulations on completing Week One of Puppy Bootcamp!

Your puppy should be well on their way in basic training—they've learned a lot this week! But remember, this is still very new to them. Make sure you keep using all of their cues with them, even if you don't continue further with training. Your puppy has only known these things for a week—or less! If you stop practicing, they won't respond as fast, and could eventually not respond at all. Use it, or they'll lose it!

To continue building on your puppy's training, you can either continue on to Week Two of Bootcamp, or you can slowly add distance, duration, and distraction to the cues you have learned this week!˙

Play Video

Scan me!

Graduation Test!

Have your puppy take this Puppy Bootcamp Week One graduation test at home!

General Cues

Sit

Cue for a Sit. Does puppy respond within 5 seconds?

Lay Down

Cue for a Lay Down while you are kneeling, then while you are standing. Does puppy respond to both?

Leave It

Ask for a Leave It. Does puppy sit back and look between your hands, waiting to be offered one?

Look

Toss a treat out. After puppy has eaten it, ask for a "Look!" Does puppy glance at you within 7 seconds?

Touch

Ask for a touch with your hand 1-2 feet away from puppy, but within their line of sight. Do they stand up and move to touch your hand with their nose?

Place

Cue puppy for Place. Do they get on the mat and stay there for at least 1 minute with intermittent rewards?

Kennel Up

Cue for a Kennel Up and point into the crate. Does puppy walk inside? When you close the door, will they Sit quietly to be let out?

Recall

When puppy is on a lead or short line 6+ feet away from you, call for a "Here!" Do they run up to you right away?

Leash Work

Take puppy for a walk. Will they walk with you without constantly stopping or bucking against it?

Food Manners

When you feed puppy, will they Sit nicely while you place the bowl down?

Socialization

Take puppy for a walk. Do they stay with you and not freeze up or cower?

Take them for a short car ride. Are they quiet and comfortable?

Take them into a small and quiet store. Are they willing to walk on their own and explore?

Have them meet a new person or dog. Do they choose to stay next to you and/or go say hi?

Set up a tunnel and a "strange" surface for them to walk over. Are they willing to try going through and over?

About the Author

Jordan grew up surrounded by dogs and fell in love with watching them learn. She's been working with puppies for over 10 years. While her pups-in-training are taking naps or working on Place, she also works as an author of fantasy and science fiction. It fits perfectly with the schedule of training! You can check out her books or short story podcast at JustBJordan.com

For free resources and to watch videos of puppies completing the Practical Puppy Bootcamp, visit PracticalPuppyTraining.com

CPSIA information can be obtained
at www.ICGtesting.com
Printed in the USA
BVHW091713250621
610384BV00017B/1411